At the Swimming Pool

Kasia Reay

Illustrated by Catherine Pape

Schofield & Sims

Dom and Amber have come for a swim. Let's visit the swimming pool with them.

Lots of <u>th</u>in<u>g</u>s fit in <u>th</u>is lo<u>ck</u>er.
Can you help Amb<u>er</u> remember
the numb<u>er</u>?

You must not run next to the pool.
You might slip and get hurt.

No running!

Armbands <u>or</u> a rubb<u>er</u> ri<u>ng</u> <u>or</u> a fl<u>oa</u>t wi<u>ll</u> help you if you cannot swim yet.

armbands

float

rubb<u>er</u> ri<u>ng</u>

swimming coach

Some children have come to the pool for a swimming test.

toddler

adult

Toddl<u>er</u>s can go in the p<u>oo</u>l t<u>oo</u>,
but they n<u>ee</u>d to be wi<u>th</u> an adult.

Some adults are bopping up and down in the pool. They come to the pool to keep fit.

fitness coach

This pool is deep, so it's for the best swimmers. Look how quick they are!

deep pool

hot shower

The hot <u>shower</u> <u>feels</u> <u>good</u>, but you must not spend <u>too</u> <u>long</u> in it.

Can you remem<u>ber</u> the numb<u>er</u> on the lo<u>ck</u><u>er</u>?

Come on, Dom! The hot <u>sh</u>ow<u>er</u> f<u>ee</u>ls g<u>oo</u>d, but you must not spend t<u>oo</u> lo<u>ng</u> in it!